JUNE IS THE FIRST FALL
© Yilong Liu
Trade Edition, 2020
ISBN 978-1-63092-129-3

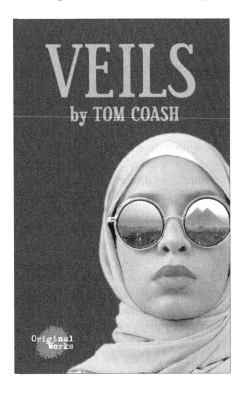

VEILS by Tom Coash

Synopsis: Intisar, a veiled, African-American Muslim student, thought she might finally fit in when she enrolled for a year abroad at the American Egyptian University in Cairo. However, the Arab Spring soon explodes across the Middle East, threatening to overwhelm the young American woman and her liberal Egyptian roommate, Samar. In the struggle to find their footing in this political storm, the young women instead find themselves on opposite sides of a bitter and dangerous cultural divide.

Cast Size: 2 Females

JUNE IS THE FIRST FALL

By
Yilong Liu

JUNE IS THE FIRST FALL had its New York premiere at New Ohio Theatre in a production produced by Yangtze Repertory Theatre of America (Chongren Fan, Artistic Director; Sally Shen, Executive Director), opening on April 5, 2019. The production was directed by Michael Leibenluft. The dramaturgy was by Gaven D. Trinidad. The set design was by Jean Kim, the costume design was by An-lin Dauber, the lighting design was by Cha See, the sound design was by Michael Costagliola, and the production stage manager was Lindsey Hurley. The cast was as follows:

DON – Alton Alburo
YU QIN – Chun Cho
DAVID – Fenton Li
JANE – Stefani Kuo
SCOTT – Karsten Otto

JUNE IS THE FIRST FALL was originally produced by Kumu Kahua Theatre (Harry Wong III, Artistic Director; Donna Blanchard, Managing Director), Honolulu, Hawaiʻi in November 2018. It was directed by Lurana Donnels O'Malley. The set design was by Sarah Danvers, the lighting design was by Cora Yamagata, the costume design was by Maile Speetjens, the sound design was by Ron Heller, the prop design was by Teia O'Malley, and the stage manager was Sarah Danvers. The cast was as follows:

DON – Adam Brading
YU QIN – Qiaoer Zheng
DAVID – Stu Hirayama
JANE – Leah M. Koeppel
SCOTT – Nicholas Myers
MATEO – Berkley Spivey

(The role of MATEO was removed prior to the New York premiere and no longer exists in this play.)

5

CHARACTERS:
YU QIN, the mother
DAVID, the father
DON, the son
JANE, the daughter
SCOTT, the boyfriend

*The family is Chinese; Scott is a local haole in Hawai'i.

PLACE:
Manoa Valley, Honolulu, Hawai'i

TIME:
a few years ago

NOTES ON LANGUAGE:
1. Dialogues in parenthesis are unsaid thoughts.

2. Yu Qin speaks Chinese/Chinglish in this play. Projection of translations won't be necessary.

"this is dialogue in Chinese/Chinglish"
"[this is English translation]"

3. "/" indicates where one character may cut in.

4. line breaks:
in general, line breaks suggest the rhythm of dialogues
if a sentence is broken down in the middle by a line break
it means I see the character taking a very slight pause
a breath
a hesitation
or searching for the right words
these pauses are not as long, rich, or loaded as a beat or
ellipses
but rather a thought map for the characters
subtle and internal

NOTES ON STYLE:
1. This piece wants to be very fluid. Transitions between scenes should be seamless. Flashback scenes are dream-like and should blend seamlessly into the present day.

2. Yu Qin is a memory/ghost. She is playful in a motherly way.

JUNE IS THE FIRST FALL

Prologue.

(A plane to Hawai'i. DON is having trouble falling asleep. YU QIN walks into his memory.)

YU QIN: 怎么了？还睡不着啊？ No sleep?
[What's the matter? Still can't sleep?]

那妈妈给你讲个故事好不好啊? A... story?
[Do you want to hear a story then?]

等你睡醒啊，我们就到夏威夷了
[When you wake up, we will be in Hawaii.]

Ha-wa-ii
Ha-waaaooorrr-ii
Ha-waaaorrrrroaroarwoof

Shhh... 你看姐姐，早就睡着啦
[Look at your sister. She fell asleep a long time ago.]

Okay. 很久很久以前啊... Once upon a time
[Once upon a time...]

天上有十个太阳
[There were ten suns in the sky.]

跟妈妈一起数好不好？
[Do you want to count with mommy?]

一个太阳One sun

两个太阳Two sun

三个太阳Three sun

四个太阳 Four sun

…

…

…

(Lights shift. She leaves his memory. Then...)

1.

(Honolulu. Afternoon. DON is with DAVID in a car.)

DAVID: You okay there?

DON: Yeah...
just
It's so hot.

DAVID: Tell me about it.
It's like an eternal summer.
Here on this island.

DON: In the car, I mean.

DAVID: Oh.
The A/C isn't working.
Here.

(DAVID rolls down the windows.

Wind.

    Wind.

        Wind.)

DON: Dad, my hair!

(*He rolls them back up a bit.*)

DAVID: Sorry. Better?

(*A nod. DON fixes his hair. They don't talk for a while. Just when it might start to feel too long...*)

DON: So... how are you?

DAVID: Good.

DON: How's the restaurant?

DAVID: Busy.
Yeah.
How was the flight?

DON: It was okay.

DAVID: That's good.

(*Another silence. Someone turns on the radio. We hear Hawaiian music.*)

DON: Where's the new place?

DAVID: Aina Haina.

DON: Why are we moving?

DAVID: We need more space.
Jane is --
...
She's such a hoarder.
And it's closer to work.

DON: I see.

DAVID: And you hated the old house.

DON: I didn't *hate* it.

DAVID: You didn't seem to like it either.

(A beat.)

DON: It just rains there all the time.

DAVID: It's called Manoa Valley, not Manoa beach.

DON: Yeah.

(Silence. Silence. Silence.)

DAVID: Well...
Welcome back.
Son.

(DON takes a deep breath.)

DON: I miss the smell of the air here.

DAVID: It's different.

DON: I miss riding in your Honda.

DAVID: Old car.

DON: I miss the music.

DAVID: Touristy crap.

DON: ... I miss you.

(A beat.)

DAVID: Yeah...
So.
You hungry?

(Lights shift.)

2.

(A house in Manoa Valley. This is a typical home in Hawai'i. Through the windows part of the clothesline in the yard can be seen. JANE is reading a book on the couch.

Rain. Rain... Rain......

She hurries to the yard to collect laundry from the clothesline.)

JANE: Fuck.
Scott?
Honey?
Can you help me?

(SCOTT enters, instead of helping her, he quickly picks up her book and pretends to read. He finds a stick of gum inside the book, peels it, and puts it in his mouth. JANE runs back holding an armful of damp sheets. She stares at him.)

JANE: Really? Since when did you start to read?

SCOTT: I read the *Star-Advertiser* every morning.

JANE: To look for coupons page by page. Help me with the laundry now!

SCOTT: Yes, sugar.

JANE: You've got to stop messing with my textbook. Now where's the part I was reading?
...
What's in your mouth?!

SCOTT: Who on earth bookmarks a page with a piece of gum?!

(JANE smacks SCOTT playfully with the book. He dodges. She chases him. He grabs her from behind and brings her down onto the couch.

A kiss.)

JANE: Hey... they'll be back any minute.
Scott...
Scott!

SCOTT: What do we have?
Five minutes?
What can we do in five minutes?

JANE: I don't know. Maybe... something hot?

SCOTT: Yeah?

JANE: And loud?

SCOTT: Yeah!

JANE: Great. So put them in the dryer now.

(She dumps the sheets on him.)

SCOTT: Borrring!

JANE: There's nothing boring about a big man doing a hot fat load of laundry.

(He picks up the sheets and sniffs.)

SCOTT: I don't get it. What's the point of having a dryer if you're just gonna hang them out every time?

JANE: I didn't know it was gonna rain like this.

SCOTT: It's Manoa, Jane, what did you think?

JANE: I like the fresh smell of sun-dried sheets. It's soothing. I want Don to have clean linen to sleep on tonight.

SCOTT: Why does he want to come back all of a sudden?

JANE: I told him about the new house.

SCOTT: But your old man was in such bad shape last year and he didn't even show up.

JANE: I'm sure New York keeps him busy.

SCOTT: I haven't seen him since he was in high school. Your mom used to make me teach him how to surf and take him on hikes, you know, to toughen him up.

JANE: And you were surprised he had a crush on you?

(A beat.)

SCOTT: How did he react when he heard about us?

JANE: ... I didn't tell him.

SCOTT: ... I thought you decided to call him?

JANE: I changed my mind.

SCOTT: Why?!

JANE: Do you know how long it has been?
He kept coming up with lame excuses to not come back.
And I didn't want to give him another reason.
I was starting to think maybe he never would.

SCOTT: You could've at least told me.
I thought we said --
I thought we were supposed to tell each other everything.

JANE: Yeah...
But this is different.
It's family.

SCOTT: I thought I was family.

JANE: You know what I meant...
Hey.
(she gives him a gentle kiss)
Now hurry, will you?

SCOTT: It's my day off, you know.

JANE: Oh, honey, I've got news for you.

SCOTT: What?

JANE: Now that you're *family*, you don't get days off. Now go.

(She smacks his butt.)

SCOTT: Damn. I want a refund. I want my ring back.

JANE: Yeah, that's gonna happen.

(They laugh. SCOTT exits. JANE looks at the engagement ring on her finger. She takes it off and puts it in her pocket. Loud car horn is heard. JANE fixes her hair, then goes to the door, anxiously waiting. DON appears with a suitcase. He is dressed like a typical New Yorker. A beat.)

JANE: Look at you...
with your tight little shirt
and fancy city shoes.
You must be so uncomfortable.

DON: Um, unlike you, I actually haven't given up on myself.
Geez, Jane, stop shopping at Ross and put on some makeup, will you?

(They laugh.)

JANE: Fuck you.

DON: I've missed you, too.

(A beat. JANE looks at DON's shoes.)

JANE: Are you gonna take those off?

(DON does. He takes a look at the house. She helps him with the suitcase.)

DON: Wow... this place hasn't changed at all...

(A beat.)

JANE: Yeah... how are you?

DON: Fine.

JANE: Yeah?

DON: Yeah. I'm fine. I'm good. Been busy.

(A beat.)

JANE: Sure...
So.
Where's Pa?

DON: He went back to the restaurant.

JANE: Does he have to? It's only Monday. How busy can it be?

DON: It's fine. I could really use some space right now.

(SCOTT enters.)

SCOTT: Oh. Hey!

DON: Hey...

(An awkward greeting.)

SCOTT: Welcome back.

DON: Yeah... right... I mean, thank you.

SCOTT: You look... um... great.

(Not really.)

JANE: You look gross. Wanna freshen up?

DON: Sure...

JANE: Would you grab him a clean towel?

SCOTT: Of course.

(He exits. A beat.)

DON: What's he doing here...?

JANE: I thought you knew we asked Scott to stick around
when Pa had that little heart attack.

DON: Was dad sick again?

JANE: He's feeling so much better now.
Scott's been extremely helpful.
The thing is... we got used to having him around.

DON: Huh? What are you saying?

JANE: He sort of lives here now... he pays rent. Well,
sort of, Pa takes it out of his paychecks --

DON: I don't understand.

JANE: He's been working at the restaurant for all these years.
Pa really likes him... thinks he's reliable.
We needed an extra pair of hands around the house.
It comes in handy.

DON: But we don't even have enough rooms.

JANE: So I made some tea. Would you like some?

DON: Wait, is he staying in my room?!

JANE: You're barely here. I got tired of dusting it for nothing, Don.

DON: I just thought
if there's a place where there'll always be a space for me
it would be... home.

JANE: Of course! I kicked him out and cleaned it for you this morning.
Your sheets are in the dryer
you know, the ones you had in high school.
Thought you might like that.

DON: You know what? Don't bother. I'll crash on the couch.

JANE: But it's already --

DON: No, really, it's cool.

JANE: Okay then...
just
get comfortable, alright?

DON: ...

JANE: Don? Are you gonna be okay?

DON: I think so.

(SCOTT enters with a towel and a shirt.)

SCOTT: Got you a clean shirt of mine, hope it fits.

DON: I've got clothes in my suitcase.

SCOTT: You look kinda wet. Just figured you may want to change into something comfortable right now.

DON: Just because it's dry doesn't mean it's comfortable. But thanks.

(DON takes the towel and exits. A moment.)

SCOTT: You told him...?

JANE: I wanted to...
I tried
But he just looks...
tired
I just don't want to upset him any further.

SCOTT: You want me to talk to him?

JANE: You crazy? Didn't you see the way he talked to you?

SCOTT: Maybe he's just being a typical New Yorker.
Maybe he's hungry.
Maybe he watched a really bad movie on the plane.

JANE: I don't know, Scott.
…
It's been ten years.

(Lights shift.)

3.

(Midnight. We can see moonlight in the dark living room. DON is upside down on the couch, staring at the sky through the window.

JANE and SCOTT enter quietly. They take off their shoes in the dark.)

DON: You can turn on the lights.

JANE: I thought you were asleep.

DON: It's six o'clock in the morning in New York. Where did you go?

JANE: I'm taking an evening class at KCC. Scott came to pick me up.

DON: What are you back in school for?

JANE: Just some basic business stuff.
It's been months since Pa had a day off.
Thought maybe I could help out more.

DON: What kind of class finishes at midnight?

SCOTT: We stopped to grab a bite.

DON: Where?

SCOTT: That cheap Korean place by Ala Moana.

JANE: I was craving meat jun.

DON: We don't have that in New York.

SCOTT: Do you want some?

DON: No. Thank you.

JANE: I think you should... you didn't really eat anything at dinner...

(JANE looks at SCOTT. SCOTT takes the food and exits into the kitchen. A silence.)

JANE: You were awfully quiet tonight.

DON: It's been a long day.

JANE: Pa got you char siu buns.
And malasadas.
So. many. malasadas!
But you barely touched them.

DON: Carbs.

JANE: Seriously?

DON: I wasn't feeling well.

JANE: Then you should get some rest.
Leave the windows open, looks like it's gonna rain.
The sound is relaxing, helps with sleep.

DON: The sound is annoying.

JANE: I like it... it's like tiny music notes from heaven.

DON: Cheesy.

JANE: You used to know all the poems
about rain.
When you were still a kid.
When we were still in China.

DON: I don't remember...

JANE: Mom made you memorize them
and perform?
Every time we had guests over?

DON: Really. I memorized all the poems?

JANE: Well, not *all* all, there's like a million of them
Just all the kiddie stuff
the easy ones
But good enough to make mom proud
I knew you didn't like it
but you knew what they meant to her
So you did it anyway
Sometimes while crying
You were so cute

DON: I'm still cute.

JANE: That's funny.

DON: Hey.

JANE: You know what's really cute?
When you finally met Pa
mom asked you to put on your little talent show
and you got so nervous that you went hiding
in the yard
We could only hear your voice shouting out the poems
But didn't know where you were
You always... like to *hide*
nobody ever knows where you are

DON: ...?

JANE: Sorry...
we won't be moving for another month
But I just get a little
nostalgic, I guess

DON: Yeah. I know
For a brief moment
on my flight back
I dreamed about
mom
telling me a story
so I could fall asleep
She loved doing that
telling us stories
Teaching us
Chinese myths
folktales
poems

JANE: Ten bucks says you can't remember any of them!

DON: But I remember thinking that she knew everything.

JANE: She did.

(A moment. Moonlight fills the room.)

DON: Then we came here, and she talked less and less, became quieter and quieter.

JANE: No, you just stopped listening to her. Two months into school all you wanted to speak was English.

DON: But do you think she was ever happy here?

JANE: Huh? ...
Of course.
Why do you ask?

DON: To know so much
so much
in Chinese
but never quite figured out English

JANE: So?... it's Hawai'i.

DON: People here still speak English.

JANE: People *here* here speak Hawaiian.
Why do you care about what people speak
On a stolen island?

DON: I can see that you really *are* taking a class at KCC.

(She hits him. They get more comfortable with each other. DAVID enters. He watches them.)

JANE: I'm just saying... Mom was fine, she had us.

DON: But what about when we were not around?
What about when we all left the house to go to school?
I kept wondering what she was doing at home all day...

DAVID: There're always plenty of things in the house that can keep an Asian mom busy all day long.

JANE: Sorry, Pa, did we wake you?

DAVID: Nah, I just had trouble falling asleep tonight, must have eaten too much.

JANE: I'll get your jacket if you'd like to take a walk outside.

DAVID: What, don't want your old man to hear you two whispering about your mother?

JANE: We just miss her.

DAVID: You know what she would say if she had heard me saying that I ate too much?

DON: What?

JANE: She'd try to give you more food.

DAVID: She'd probably ask, "Stomachache? Want me make you congee? "

JANE: And you'd say no but she'd make it anyway.

DAVID: And leave a huge bowl right in front of me no matter where I go.

JANE: Until someone eats it.

DON: Two times that happened!

(They all laugh. A soft moment. SCOTT enters with the take-out box. He doesn't want to intrude on this moment.)

SCOTT: Sorry to intrude... I heated up some meat jun for you.

(He leaves the food on the table.)

DON: Thanks. I really appreciate it.

SCOTT: You got it.

DAVID: Kanekoa...

SCOTT: Yeah?

DAVID: Could you let the restaurant know that I'll be in a bit late tomorrow?

SCOTT: Not feeling well...?

DAVID: Nah, just wanna take the kids to see their mother.

SCOTT: Oh, of course, I'll let them know.

DAVID: She'll be so happy to see you, Don. After all, it's almost our Mid-Autumn Festival.

DON: *(a realization)* Oh, right...

SCOTT: The Moon Festival? When people eat mooncakes?

DAVID: That's the one.

SCOTT: Isn't it usually in September?

JANE: Yes.

SCOTT: But it's only the start of June now.

JANE: That's how we like it.

SCOTT: Okay...
...
Are you gonna tell me why?

JANE: *(teasingly)* No... it's not the time.

(JANE's words trigger something in DON. He remembers his mother.)

DON: Is that...?

JANE: What?

DON: Didn't mom used to say that?
When we --
Nothing, never mind.
I just... have a headache... I think.

JANE: We'll get out of your way then... it's late, get some sleep.

DON: Good night...

JANE: Eat something first, okay?

(DON nods. They exit. He looks at the food. He has no appetite.

Lights start to shift.

The mother, YU QIN, walks into his memory... She chases him and tries to feed him food with chopsticks.)

YU QIN: 吃呀, 怎么又不吃了？ Eat more!
[How come you stop eating again?]

你看人家阿真，早就吃光了！
[Look at Jane, she finished eating long ago!]

你吃这么少，怎么长得高？
[How can you get any taller if you keep eating so little?]

以后像你爹那么矮怎么办？
[What are you going to do if you turn out to be short like your father?]

Pretty girls like tall boys.

Ugh, where you go? Finish your rice! Huh? What you mean no room?

就知道不该给你买零食！晚饭都吃不下。
[I know I shouldn't have bought you snacks. Now you have no room for dinner.]

Stomachache? Aiya, eat too fast...

You want congee.

(She hums the tune of the song Fly Me To The Moon quietly. She leaves. Lights shift.)

4.

(A cemetery in Manoa Valley. DAVID, DON, and JANE are on stage. DON holds a bouquet of daisies. JANE hums the same tune of Fly Me to The Moon softly. DON looks at her.)

29

DON: That's...?

JANE: Her favorite song.

DON: Yeah?

JANE: She used to sing you to sleep with it.
It was the *first* English song we've ever heard in China.
They played it on the radio once and she *loved* it.
We waited for almost two hours for it to play again the next day.

DON: That does sound like something she would do.

DAVID: You were only five when you got here.
Has it been that long already?
Feels like yesterday
when I drove to the airport
the first time you all arrived in Hawai'i...
You were crying so hard.

DON: I was?

JANE: Because of all the Chinese food the Customs made us throw away.

DAVID: And "the scary man" picking you up over his shoulder.

DON: I never called you scary.

JANE: Then why were you screaming like a little girl?

DON: I don't know! Maybe it's not necessarily fun for any kid to be carried on the shoulder after a long plane ride?

DAVID: I was excited to finally hold you again. When I left, you were still this baby who couldn't stop sucking his own toes.

…

I bet I can still do it. I bet I can still carry you on my back.

DON: Huh?

JANE: No way, Pa. That's crazy.

DAVID: Don't believe me? Come on. Try.

DON: What? No, dad.

JANE: It's dangerous, Pa.

DAVID: It's fun.

DON: It's stupid!

DAVID: Come on.

DON: Dad. Stop it!
Seriously.
Dad. Dad. Dad!
People are watching!
You're embarrassing me!

(A loaded beat.)

DAVID: Sure, you think *this* is embarrassing
in public
for you
but when you came out to everybody
in *my* restaurant --

JANE: Pa.

DAVID: ...
...
I'll be in the car.

(He exits.)

DON: What the fuck was that??

JANE: He was just trying to recreate a moment that meant something to him.

DON: By treating me like a kid?!

JANE: He doesn't know how to talk to you like an adult. You never gave him a chance to...
running off to college on the East Coast like that.

DON: You heard him. I knew he still can't get over the fact that I'm gay.

JANE: But he never stopped trying to.

DON: Like you would know.

JANE: Who do you think was the one who stuck around when you just ran away?

DON: I didn't run away.

JANE: You didn't stay, either.

DON: I couldn't! He hates me!

JANE: Don't be crazy.

DON: Then maybe he should! I know I would if I were him --

JANE: Are you still thinking about that?

DON: If I didn't fight with her that night, she wouldn't have stormed out; if she didn't leave the house, she would never have --

JANE: It was an accident. Okay? We've been over this. It wasn't your fault.

DON: But does he think so too?

JANE: Of course!

DON: When I was sleeping on the couch
all I could think about was
the last thing she said to me...
"But you are a man."

(A beat.)

JANE: Maybe it's good we're moving then...

(It rains.)

DON: I fucking hate Hawai'i.

JANE: No one hates Hawai'i.

DON: I do. I do I do I do.

JANE: Do you need a moment...?

(He nods. She exits. DON picks petals off the flowers. A shift...

Flower petals fall from the sky around him. Sounds of a thousand Chinese poems echo in the air. Time and space transform. We look into the past. In this memory, DON is maybe only three.

Little JANE enters. DON hides.)

JANE: Why are you hiding here? Mommy's looking for you.

DON: I'm not ready...

JANE: But you have to memorize them by dinner.
Cousins are coming.
So are their moms.
They are mean.
If you can't recite them
They'll laugh at ya.

DON: Too many words!

JANE: You're not trying hard enough.

DON: You do it then.

JANE: You're smart.

DON: But you're older. You're six.

JANE: Exactly.
It's not as impressive when I do it.
And I'm a girl.

DON: So what?

JANE: So
Poems don't do shit for me
I just need to look pretty

DON: Who said that??

JANE: Auntie.

DON: Which one??

JANE: I don't know.
They all look the same.
They have the same makeup.

DON: That's unfair...

JANE: Do you want me to put lipstick on you?

DON: Why?

JANE: So you'll look pretty too.

DON: No.
Well.
Maybe later.

JANE: Maybe it will be easier
if you understand
what the poem is saying.

DON: Mom said it's
It rained when I was asleep
And I woke up
And find my flowers dead on the ground.

JANE: And?

DON: And I'm sad.

JANE: So you do understand what it means.

DON: But I don't know why.

JANE: Why the person is sad?

DON: No, why I need to recite them?

JANE: So people will know you're smart.

DON: Why do people need to know I'm smart?

JANE: So dad might be happy when he sees you?
He's smart too.
He's the smartest person in the world.

DON: But where is he?

JANE: America?

DON: Where is that?

JANE: ...I don't know.

DON: Ask mom.

JANE: I did!

DON: What did she say?

JANE: She said, here.

(Little JANE sticks out a finger and touches little DON's heart.

Lights shift. We are back in the present.

The cemetery. DON regards the grave.)

5.

(It's early in the morning. DON is going through a box of his old stuff. Old clothes mostly, maybe there's a pair of muddy yellow shoes in there. He is trying on old clothes to see which ones to keep in this scene.

SCOTT runs in. He has just come back from jogging. He is shirtless. He wipes his sweat off, then stretches some more in the yard. Soon he realizes DON is in the room, so he puts his shirt back on.)

SCOTT: It's lovely outside.
(no response)
Maybe next time you could come running with me.
(no response)
It may help with your jet lag.

DON: Maybe.

SCOTT: Sorting out old stuff?
Jane doesn't want me to touch any of it.
Don't know what's important to you and what's not.

DON: Feels nice to clean. Really brings back some high school memories.

SCOTT: / Good times.

DON: Tough times.

SCOTT: At least you're making it in the bad-ass city!
I'm still stuck in the same place
working my ass off for your dad.

DON: I'm sure he treats you well.
The haole guy working in a Chinese restaurant
how often does that happen?
You're his lucky charm.
Hell, you're like the Japanese money cat!
Your very existence is just shouting out "come in, come in" to people.

(SCOTT waves his arm up and down like the Japanese lucky cat.)

SCOTT: *(in a cat-like cartoonish voice)* "Come in, come in"
our veggies are not frozen
and we're not trying to pass off anything as chicken!

(They laugh.)

DON: You're so bad.

SCOTT: Got you to laugh.

DON: You still got it, still crack me up.

SCOTT: You look like you could use a couple of jokes...
Let me know if you ever feel up for a run.
You'll feel better.
We can go to Magic Island.

DON: Sure. I do miss
nature.
Hey...

SCOTT: Yeah?

DON: Did you ever finish... Ka'au Crater?

SCOTT: Oh.
That's...
not an easy hike.

DON: Too bad we only got to the third waterfall... I kept
wondering what it's like after that.

SCOTT: Maybe it's not that different.

DON: But what if it is -- weren't you at least curious?

SCOTT: I guess not. Plenty other hikes that are less risky,
but just as beautiful.

DON: I never stopped thinking about it.

SCOTT: It's dangerous to go back...
especially in the rainy season.
…
You could get hurt.

DON: Big deal.

SCOTT: Huh?

(A beat.)

DON: Nothing. Never mind.

*(DON goes back to the box of old clothes. He takes out an
old shirt. It looks funny.)*

DON: Do you think this still fits?

SCOTT: Totally.

(DON tries it on.)

DON: Well?

SCOTT: Keep it. Wear it in New York.

DON: And kiss my social life goodbye.

SCOTT: Oh. I've never been to New York. I've never even left Hawai'i.

DON: Maybe you just haven't found a good reason to.

SCOTT: You know what's the one thing that I really wanna do, if I ever had a chance to visit?

DON: Catch a Broadway musical? Take a break from the Pidgin and hula shows?

SCOTT: No, I... I really just wanna see a squirrel.

DON: *(laughing)* A squirrel?

SCOTT: What! I've never seen one. We don't have any of those here, and they're so damn cute!

DON: I get it. I totally went crazy over those little guys in my first year. Hell, I think I still do. Sometimes I'd go to the park just to throw cashews on the ground and watch them go nuts.

SCOTT: That sounds epic!

DON: Yeah, epic squirrel fights!
My friend loves them too.
I mean, he won't go crazy over them, but his twin daughters...

they just won't go home until all the squirrels are gone.
One time I was with them in Washington Square Park.
It was after take-your-kids-to-work day.
I bought them ice cream.
But they just ran off chasing some squirrels then
fell asleep on their father's shoulder...

SCOTT: That's so sweet.

DON: Then the sun went down, he took them home, and I just sat there by myself, finishing their ice cream cones.

SCOTT: Oh...

DON: You know, the color of the sunset that day was really beautiful, like something was burning on fire.

SCOTT: Aren't all sunsets like that?

DON: Something's always different each day.

SCOTT: Cool. I didn't know that. Guess I was never patient enough.

DON: No, you weren't.
But you don't have to be.
Who pays attention to the sky, when he has someone to talk to?

(Lights shift.)

6.

(In a car. DAVID is looking at the sky while driving. JANE is going over their bank statements.)

JANE: Keep your eyes on the road, Pa.

41

DAVID: Mmm... yeah.

JANE: Do you want me to drive?

DAVID: No, just... um, do your thing. I got this.

JANE: *(sarcastically)* Yeah, you're really on top of stuff.

DAVID: What's that supposed to mean?

JANE: We are losing money.
Maybe it's time to open again for those afternoon hours?
You feeling a lot better, no?

DAVID: Yeah... but
I'm getting used to having a break then so I can
take a nap
or just
It's kinda nice.

JANE: Well, then let him help.
Let Scott do something.
Just because you have to sleep doesn't mean we have to
close.

DAVID: He is doing something.

JANE: Let him do something important.

DAVID: Well, he's taking care of you.

JANE: Aww. Nice try.

DAVID: What! I mean it.

JANE: Then trust him.

(A small beat.)

DAVID: It's not that I don't trust --
I just like being there...
He's a very nice kid.

JANE: You don't even let us live in the same room.

DAVID: That's different.... he sneaks out during the middle of the night anyway.

JANE: You don't have a problem with Don not living there for ten years but you can't stand my boyfriend sneaking out to see me for ten minutes?

DAVID: Ten minutes... Come on, give that kid more credit.

JANE: I'm serious! Sometimes I feel...

DAVID: What?

JANE: Nothing...
It's just
I mean...
...
...
You don't even buy *me* malasadas...

(A small beat. Maybe DAVID laughs a little. He finds this silly.)

DAVID: That's what this is about...?
I'm buying us a new house, aren't I?
what do you think it is for?
I just think

43

When you start a new family
You deserve
a new place
a fresh start
I bought our place in Manoa when we...
When I...
It's worth waiting for.

(A silence.)

JANE: You know you're gonna have to talk to him some time, right?

DAVID: You know you're gonna have to talk to him some time, too, yah?

JANE: He thinks you hate him.

DAVID: Hate him?!

JANE: Are you really surprised, after all that happened?

(A small beat.)

DAVID: Do you know why he flew back this time, after all these years?

JANE: He didn't say anything... He's more like you than you realize.

(Silence. DAVID keeps driving. He looks up at the sky. He sees something.)

JANE: Pa.

DAVID: Yeah?

JANE: You missed my exit.

(Lights shift.)

7.

(DON is smoking a bowl. He looks comfortable. He's wearing something much more comfortable too. He is on his phone. We can't see what he's doing but he's probably on Grindr.

Message alert. Okay, he's definitely on Grindr.

Car approaches. He drops his phone and tries to cover up the smell in all sorts of ways.

DAVID comes in. DON is trying to act natural. But it's not coming off that way.

A comical silence.)

DAVID: ... it's late, you ate?

DON: Yes, daddy.
(fuck)
Dad. Yes, dad.
I did.
I ate.

(Wild message alerts! DON's phone is on the ground, somewhere close to DAVID. DAVID picks it up. He looks at it: huh, oh, wow.)

DON: Um, it's like, Facebook, but, for, guys.

DAVID: But
they don't have
faces.

DON: That's because
it's Hawai'i
why don't I just

(He takes the phone back.)

DAVID: What do you mean "because it's Hawai'i"?

DON: It's just
too small.
everybody knows everybody.
most people are still
closeted--
scared
of being
caught
found out
before they are ready to
...

(DAVID takes this in.)

DAVID: Your sister once signed me up for something
too.

DON: She did not!

DAVID: A stupid idea but
yeah...
everybody looked familiar
I didn't know all of them...
But when we started talking

we very quickly realized how many friends we have in
common
...

DON: That's what I'm talking about.

DAVID: And after a while
they just hit me up with
take-out orders

(DON laughs.)

DON: *(high AF)* That's legit.
...
I mean
they know that's what you do
so
it's just a good ice breaker

DAVID: I guess.

DON: People do that
like
for us
it's always
A first date question
To share
your
coming out story
You think I...
I don't even know how to...

(A beat.)

DAVID: Look... about the other day...

DON: It's fine.
I'm good.
Really.

DAVID: I just need you to know that... I'm happy you're
here.

DON: Yeah...
I know...
Me too
The rainbow state...
It's so
Ironic...

(A beat.)

DAVID: You think it was easy for me back in the day?
With all the beautiful wahine on the island, I told your
grandpa that I met your mother on my trip to China and I
wanted to marry her. You think he was happy?

DON: I never got to see him.

DAVID: He worked too hard, left us the year before you
got here. We had nothing before, Don. He was a busboy in
Chinatown, always dreamed about one day having our
own restaurant. When we finally did, he was so proud that
he handwrote our very first menu in Chinese. Every single
copy of it.
(beat; tenderly)
He was the nicest man, but he was also secretly rooting
for me and this Filipino girl, Danita.

DON: I never heard you talk about this.

DAVID: Because your mother would hit me with a ladle if I did.

DON: *(laughing)* She wouldn't!

DAVID: I just couldn't see myself spending the rest of my life with a "Danita", you know? Danita Qín. Didn't feel right. She couldn't even say it, she couldn't say our family name, "Qín".

DON: "Chín."

DAVID: "Qín."

DON: "Chín."

DAVID: Qín Yǔ-Qín.

DON: "Chín Yu-Chín."

DAVID: You can't say it, either! You can't even say your mom's name correctly. Forgot all your Chinese?

DON: Sound the same to me!

DAVID: No, they really don't. I love her name. When it comes to Chinese names, every single character could have dozens of different meanings. Combining with any other characters, they create hundreds and thousands of meanings. Only when you say a name correctly, can you see the meaning behind it.
(beat)
Still remember what her name means?

DON: I know "yu" is the rain.

49

DAVID: Any three-year old in China knows it's the rain.

DON: I never learned how to write the characters of her name.

DAVID: You never wanted to learn to write / at all.

DON: I could understand you guys most of the time / anyway.

DAVID: But I've always hoped you could help with our business when I get old. Well, I got old.

DON: It's a nice restaurant, I'm sure that --

DAVID: It's the *best* restaurant. The only place to get a plate of / decent Chinese food in Aina Haina.

DON: ...decent Chinese food in Aina Haina. I know. I know! I was just never interested in running a restaurant.

DAVID: *(suddenly, a bit resentful)* Can you even read the menu?! Huh? Can you?

DON: Dad...?

(DAVID quickly collects himself.)

DAVID: *(faking laughs)* Well, who am I to give Chinese lessons? You must be bored to tears by me! Should I get you some tea?

DON: No.

DAVID: Good. More for me.

DON: Dad, let me.

DAVID: No. No, you stay here.
Don't leave.
I got this. Just stay here.
Don't go.
(beat)
Don't leave.

(DAVID exits. DON doesn't move, until we see...)

8.

(A pair of muddy shoes falls from the sky. The hike. Ka'au Crater. DON is seventeen.)

SCOTT: Hey.
Don.
Come on.
We've got a long way to go.
Keep up!

DON: What fresh hell is this, Kanekoa?
I said a *fun* hike.
We're in the middle of a jungle!

SCOTT: A *crater*. Isn't that fun?

DON: Look at my shoes.
My mom's gonna kill me.
She'll never get this mud off.
Should've just gone to the beach...
and read a book.

SCOTT: Stop being such a dork
just do what I do
just take your shoes off

DON: They're ruined anyway.
Thanks.
My dad is so gonna give me the look.

SCOTT: The look.

DON: Yeah, like
when he looks at you
but doesn't say anything
that's the worst
because you don't know
what exactly you did wrong
so you just replay all the shitty things
in your head
punishing yourself

SCOTT: Classic. Ha. Your dad sucks.

DON: Yeah. Totally.

SCOTT: I was kidding.

DON: I was not.

(A small beat.)

SCOTT: Do you need anything? A break? Water? Sunscreen?

DON: Yeah...

(DON stops to drink some water. He takes out a bottle of sunscreen from his bag. He puts sunscreen on his face and neck. There is a smudge left on his face.)

SCOTT: So... not close with your dad, huh?

DON: Everyone hates their dad. Don't you?

SCOTT: I'm adopted.

DON: ...

SCOTT: I wish I knew who he was.
Maybe I could hate him.
Yeah.
Maybe I do.
But can you really hate someone you never know?

DON: I didn't really know who my dad was when I was a kid either.

SCOTT: How's that possible?

DON: He met my mom
on one of his trips to China.
Then he had to leave.
To come back here.
All I could see was a picture of him.

SCOTT: Still.
He's here.
You're here.

DON: But I never feel
quite like myself
In front of him
Or in front of anybody...

(A beat. SCOTT notices the smudge.)

SCOTT: You missed a spot.

(SCOTT gestures, but DON touches the wrong side of his face. SCOTT goes to help DON. He gently wipes the smudge off DON's face.)

SCOTT: There.

DON: Thanks...
(a beat)
Do *you* ever feel
there are two versions of yourself
and you try so hard to be both
But end up being neither?

SCOTT: Sorta...
I grew up here but no one believes I'm local.
In school all the racist Filipino kids call me stupid haole.
(in Pidgin)
"Eh Kanekoa, how come you white but your last name Hawaiian?
What? Your maddah one whore?
How come your skin come pink in da sun like one pig? "

DON: Sorry...

SCOTT: It's fine. I'm used to it...

DON: It's just...
sometimes
I don't really know
Who I... am

SCOTT: Well... then
who do you wanna be?
I'm just thinking

54

They didn't take you all the way here
For you not to be
you
…
I like to think like that
for myself too
That maybe they had to give me up because

(A beat.)

DON: Hey.

SCOTT: Yeah?

DON: You hungry?

SCOTT: No?

DON: I have char siu buns.

SCOTT: Ew. Who packs that for a hike?

DON: My mom.
Well
Because
If you are
You can have mine

SCOTT: Yeah.
Sure.
Thanks...
(a soft moment)
Well.
Let's get moving.
We're almost at the first waterfall!

DON: I can hear it.

SCOTT: Ready to clamber up?

DON: Yeah!
Wait.
What?

SCOTT: The waterfall.
There are ropes there.
We have to climb it to get to the crater!

DON: I don't want to do that.

SCOTT: *(jokingly; in Pidgin)* No can, brah
Your maddah's order
Gotta toughen you up!

(SCOTT walks away. DON watches him.

The memory of YU QIN comes in and she watches DON.

Reality cracks a little.

A moment...

DON follows SCOTT out...

They disappear into the hike.)

9.

*(JANE is getting the house ready for the moon festival.
Car horn is heard. A moment later, SCOTT enters with a
box of mooncakes. She takes the box and studies it care-
fully. Then, she gives him a look. The same look her father
has.)*

JANE: I asked for mooncakes.

SCOTT: This is mooncake.

JANE: This is some Japanese matcha shit.

SCOTT: Yeah, matcha mooncakes.

JANE: Who wants mooncakes that taste like green tea, when you're supposed to eat them while having tea?

SCOTT: I don't know, the Japanese?

JANE: Scott!

SCOTT: You go get it then. This is Hawai'i, everything has Japanese written all over it. Besides, where am I supposed to find mooncakes, when it's not even the Moon Festival?

JANE: Chinatown?

SCOTT: Are they even fresh?

JANE: At least they would look like the real thing.

SCOTT: What's the big deal? It's not even the real Mid-Autumn Festival. Who cares?

JANE: I care! Does that mean anything to you?

SCOTT: Of course it does!

JANE: Then do something.

SCOTT: Do you really want to do this right now?

JANE: I asked you for *one* thing and you can't even --

SCOTT: I miss you!

JANE: What?!

SCOTT: I miss you, Jane!
Sorry if I got the wrong thing.
I just wanted to get it over with so I could come back and spend time with you.
I feel like I haven't seen you for days.

JANE: Don hasn't been back for Mid-Autumn for years...
We never celebrated it after he left.
It's one of the most important family holidays, you know?

(A beat.)

SCOTT: Fine. I'll go to Chinatown.

(He starts to leave. She stops him and touches his chest and arms in a loving way.)

JANE: Thank you.

SCOTT: *(sighing)* Anything, for you.

(He kisses her, then exits. She watches him leave.

DON enters a moment later with a notebook.

He scares her from behind. She is caught off-guard.)

DON: Every time.

JANE: You little rascal!

DON: I can't believe that still works on you.

JANE: I can't believe you're still doing it!

DON: Well, you should know, I've been coming from behind for a while.

JANE: Ew! Where's that little brother I knew who used to blush at dirty jokes?

DON: Let's just say no one can survive New York without getting a little dirty. Dad left?

JANE: No, that was Scott.

DON: Where did he go?

JANE: I asked him to get us a little something.

DON: "Fetch. Good boy."

JANE: Stupid.

DON: God, how long has he been working for us?

JANE: *Long.*

DON: When we first met him, I was only sixteen, I think.

JANE: Right, and I was having second thoughts about college.

DON: Isn't it just adorable? Two college dropouts. You and him?

JANE: Shut up. You know why I dropped out.

(A small beat.)

DON: Yeah...
that was...
thanks
how is it?
you like it?
School?

JANE: feels good to finally do something for myself...

DON: What else is new with you?

JANE: Huh...?

DON: What?

JANE: You almost never... I can't remember the last time you asked me that.

DON: Ever since I started cleaning
putting things into boxes
I just been seeing these
moments
memories
of us
popping out
from everywhere
I don't know if I was dreaming or if I was...
don't you feel weird
that every version of ourselves
probably still exist somewhere in this house?

(JANE notices the notebook.)

JANE: Have you been practicing Chinese?! I thought you hated it!!

DON: I never *hated* it... I just
I just never felt like myself in the language
Yes, Chinese is great
It's old it's poetic it's beautiful it's whatever
But there's not even a right word for gay

JANE: There is --

DON: But it sounds like a disease
a dysfunction
a defect
The only thing people could say was
"I like guys"

(A beat.)

JANE: We are subtle people.

DON: *(laughs)* You know, dad caught me smoking and...
yeah.

JANE: Did he say anything?

DON: No. He just told me about a time when he was
young...
And I feel we...
...
Bonded?
Ugh... that's so cheesy...

JANE: See? He loves you.

DON: Wouldn't hurt to actually say it once in a while.

JANE: He doesn't need to say it. It's so obvious.

DON: I just want to hear it. I just want to feel the words.

(Beat.)

JANE: When I was going through your closet to find the sheets you slept on in high school, I saw the magazine. The dirty magazine I gave you.

DON: The Playboy? It still weirds me out a little even to this day thinking you would buy something like that for me.

JANE: Well, I didn't. It wasn't me who bought it, Don. It was Pa. He just asked me to pass it to you.

DON: Huh? That doesn't make it any less weird. Even more so, if anything.

JANE: My point is, he never stopped wanting to help you.

DON: By giving a gay kid a Playboy magazine?

JANE: Maybe he wanted you to figure things out.

DON: I most certainly did. Those huge... tits did nothing but assure me / I am gay.

JANE: Let's not get graphic. All I'm saying is... give Pa a chance to get to know you.

DON: I don't know, Jane...

JANE: He is tougher than you think.

DON: You sure?

JANE: Yeah.

DON: Jane?

JANE: Yeah?

(A beat.)

DON: Are you happy?

JANE: Why...? Anything wrong?

DON: No. Just want to make sure you're happy.

JANE: I am. Is that all you want to know?

DON: Yeah.
Actually, there *is* one more thing.
Can you teach me how to write mom's name in Chinese?

(A small beat. She nods. Lights shift.)

10.

(DON is practicing writing. He can't get it right. YU QIN walks in...)

YU QIN: 写啊，怎么不写了？
[Keep writing! Why did you stop?]

What you stare me for? 我脸上又没有写字儿。
[There are no answers written on my face, are there?]

What? Too hard? Of course! 不然呢？你以为这是什么
啊？菲律宾话？
[So? What do you think this is? Tagalog?]

现在不练习写字，等你长大就更难了。
[If you don't practice writing now, it will only get harder
as you grow up.]

*(She pantomimes the waves of the Chinese character
"rain" in the air. We feel the words.)*

横！别以为我在吓你。竖！以后你再看中文跟鬼画符
一样的时候... 勾！别来找我哭。
[Horizontal stroke! I'm not scaring you. Vertical stroke!
Don't come crying to me if one day... hook stroke... Chinese looks like alien doodles to you!]

*(DON repeats the movement. He says the following line in
bold with her but in English.)*

多会一门语言，就是多一双看世界的眼睛。
**[To know a second language is to have another pair of
eyes to see the world.]**

你的世界只会越来越大，我不希望你忘了我的呀。
[Your world is going to get bigger and bigger, but I don't
want you to forget mine.]

Finish.

Let me see.

Hmm. Good.

(YU QIN leaves. DAVID enters. He sees the notebook.)

DAVID: Not bad.

DON: Dad! You scared me.

DAVID: Let me take a look.

DON: No, it's embarrassing.

DAVID: Only if you got it wrong.

DON: Dad!

DAVID: I'm joking. Show me, will you?

DON: But remember, I just started.

DAVID: This one over here looks neat.

DON: That's Jane's handwriting!

DAVID: Oh.

DON: Mine's at the bottom of the page.

DAVID: ...Still good.

DON: Who am I kidding? It looks like... alien doodles.

DAVID: Better than nothing, right?

(A beat.)

DAVID: You want a beer?

DON: *(not really)* ... sure.

(DAVID goes to get two beers.)

DAVID: I was in Kailua today. Oh boy I haven't been on that side of the island for ages! How strange, that it always seemed so far, but it only took me less than twenty minutes to get there. It got me thinking, is that really how small this island is? I didn't realize that before, people were much more patient back in my day. We'd wait for weeks for letters to deliver, months or even years to kiss a girl.

DON: World is changing fast.

DAVID: It's making people want more.

DON: Not necessarily a bad thing...

DAVID: No, wanting is good, but not knowing when to stop is dangerous. You know, I traveled a lot too when I was young, never wanted to settle down, until I met your mother. You're still young, son. Maybe Hawai'i… *is* too small for you.

DON: I used to think that, too. I used to think maybe Hawai'i is not right for me, it drags me down... but now, I feel like I've reached a point of my life where things aren't ever getting better… like I'm climbing up a mountain, once I've reached the top, everything after that is just going downhill.

(A beat.)

DAVID: How is it, with New York?

DON: Same old.

DAVID: If it's same old, then why are you back here in Hawai'i?

DON: I don't know. No reason.

DAVID: There's always a reason when someone misses home... How is New York?

DON: It's a city where no one ever wants to settle down.

DAVID: You ready for that?

DON: Perhaps.

(Beat.)

DAVID: Tell me about him.

DON: I'm not sure if this is something you'd take interest in.

DAVID: Well, I am asking, aren't I?
(beat)
When I woke up in The Queen's Medical Center, after... that heart attack, you know what I was thinking? I was thinking, how I almost left this world, without knowing who you really are, without knowing what -- or who -- makes you happy. And that... was what really scared me.
(beat)
What's he like?

DON: ... He's Italian.

DAVID: Fancy.

DON: Italian American from Brooklyn.

DAVID: Still good.

DON: He has a slight accent, one that people can hardly tell, but I make fun of it all the time.

DAVID: Of course you do.

DON: I met him one summer, a year after I graduated college, at a coffee shop around NYU.

DAVID: He likes coffee, huh? Let me guess, does he also like pizza, spaghetti, and pasta?

DON: Dad!

DAVID: What? Only they can say stereotypes about us?

DON: He was there to get coffee... and yes he had a slice of pizza for lunch.

DAVID: *(chuckling)* Go on.

DON: I was in line for the bathroom... Some homeless guy was taking forever, and I just couldn't hold it any longer. Together we cursed the guy that was hogging the restroom.

DAVID: I heard that's a popular way for people to bond in New York.

DON: Then we laughed, and he asked me if I would want to walk to his office to use their bathroom.

DAVID: Why was he even waiting in line in the first place if he could just go back and --

DON: I don't know, dad.

DAVID: Maybe he just wanted to talk to you.

DON: I'd like to think that.

DAVID: And you did go with him?

DON: Yeah. His office was right there by Washington Square Park, just next to the Arch. He works at NYU.

DAVID: *(a bit impressed)* Oh.

DON: Then we got to talk. I told him his accent was charming, and he thought the little dance I did when I really had to pee was funny. One thing led to another, he asked me if I'd like to go to a museum with him that weekend.

DAVID: Museum? And they say Italians are romantic.

DON: He had free tickets from work.

DAVID: NYU is a nice school.

DON: Yeah.

DAVID: Does he teach?

DON: No.

DAVID: What does he do then?

DON: He advises students from other countries. China. Vietnam. Japan...

DAVID: Still good.

DON: I guess.

DAVID: So what's the issue?

DON: We don't think it's working out anymore.

DAVID: Oh. What a shame. NYU is a nice school.

DON: Yeah.

DAVID: Is he nice to you?

DON: He is, but… it's complicated, he also has other things to take care of.

DAVID: So? He doesn't have time for a…
boyfriend?
What's so complicated?

DON: Summer school...

DAVID: Summer school?

DON: Yeah.

DAVID: Well, that's just idiotic... fighting over work --

DON: His daughters' summer school.
(beat)
He's married with kids…
To his husband
It was *working* for the three of us
…
We went traveling
His husband brought his mother
And I heard him calling his husband's mom… mom

And I just felt…
that's something I can never
And I wanted more
I want what they have
Then…

(A long silence.)

DAVID: I thought NYU was a nice school.

(DAVID slowly walks away.

He stops.

A long and painful look.

He exits.

Something breaks inside DON.

He smashes the beer can on the ground.

Lights shift.)

11.

(JANE remembers her mother as she prepares for the moon festival. YU QIN enters from the past. They help each other set the plates down, cut mooncakes, and places little paper lanterns on the wall.)

YU QIN: 很久很久以前，天上有十个/太阳。
[Once upon a time, there was ten suns / in the sky.]

JANE: Once upon a time, there were ten suns in the sky
scorching the earth and turning the world into a wasteland
Out of the madness, a young man stepped up.
He climbed on top of the tallest mountain
and shot nine of the suns out the sky.

YU QIN: One sun...
two suns...
three suns...
/ four suns...

JANE: to thank him for his bravery
people made him the king of their land
but he soon grew drunk with power
One day, he got the elixir of life from the gods
But before he could take it
his wife stole it and left
she just knew she couldn't let a tyrant rule forever
Trying to flee, she swallowed the pill, and jumped out the
window --
But instead of falling, she found herself...

YU QIN: Flying...

JANE: higher and higher and higher / and higher.

YU QIN: All the way, to the moon.

*(The rest of the family enters. They sit around the table in
silence.)*

JANE: When people find out what happened
they gazed at the moon in the sky
and when it was at its brightest and fullest
the silhouette looked just like her...
so they made mooncakes

her favorite
to remember her.

Sometimes leaving may feel like flying
Sometimes flying may seem like falling
but we won't know until we do it.

*(A moment. YU QIN leaves. JANE watches her. Lights
shift, then...)*

12.

*(Night. The family is sitting quietly, having mooncakes.
No one is talking for a very long time.)*

SCOTT: This mooncake is so good.
(no one responds)
I like the salted yolk in the middle.
(no one responds)
So... it's supposed to represent the moon
(no one responds)
...as the moon will be at its brightest and fullest at Mid-
Autumn Day --

JANE: Yes, that's correct.

SCOTT: Shame it's not full moon tonight.

JANE: Just eat.

DAVID: It's a family tradition.

SCOTT: To celebrate Moon Festival early?

DAVID: It's her mother's idea.

SCOTT: Because...?

JANE: Because mooncakes are cheaper when you buy them early.

(SCOTT laughs. DON stares at him.)

DON: Because this is the day we first arrived in Hawai'i...

SCOTT: Oh?

JANE: We never celebrated Mid-Autumns back in China...

SCOTT: Why not?

JANE: It may seem fun.
Mooncakes, lanterns...
But the idea of the festival is really just simple -- it's a family day.

DAVID: It's like Thanksgiving. People travel home to be with their families, no matter where they are.

JANE: Just instead of slaughtering turkeys, we appreciate the grace of the moon while enjoying mooncakes.

DON: But we did nothing back in China. She kept saying it wasn't the time.

JANE: Because Pa wasn't there.

SCOTT: I see, wouldn't be a family day without him.

JANE: But we had a huge banquet the night we flew in. Pa invited everyone he knew. Mom was so happy. She even drank a little!

DON: I've never seen her drunk.

JANE: Me neither before that! She was so fun when she got tipsy. Everyone was cheering, asking her to sing a song, and she did! She even climbed up on the chair and sang like a super star. Then she declared, while holding another drink in hand, that today is the day -- our very own Mid-Autumn Festival.

DAVID: Because we were finally together.

JANE: She asked where she could get mooncakes. People were laughing at her.

DAVID: It was the hottest day of June that year.

JANE: They said it's summer in Hawai'i all year round, they said there's no fall in paradise. But she didn't care, she told them we've waited long enough -- if there's no autumn, she'll start the first one! So we got used to celebrating Mid-Autumn this time every year.

SCOTT: Wow. That's an incredible story.

JANE: It is. She had a few drinks and started talking to us in really good English.

DON: Mom, speaking in good English...?

JANE: It was the alcohol. Well, most of what she said was just direct translations from Chinese which made little sense, but they sounded good!

DAVID: *(remembering)* Yeah... "Moon no round okay, as long as mooncakes round."

JANE: "Today hot to death, just like spicy sauce."

DAVID: "Who says no fall here? June is the first fall then!"

JANE: *(laughing)* Then Pa asked her, "You want to be the first to fall, huh?", so he shook her chair and she fell right into his arms.

(They laugh. They remember the past when --)

DON: How cute -- the "story" you just told.

(A beat.)

JANE: You were tiny. You were probably stuffed from eating all that char siu buns and fell asleep.

DON: You know what I do remember about that night? A room filled with obnoxious strangers, drinking and shouting.

JANE: Celebrating, for us. We deserved a little break after our long trip.

DON: Yeah, from being dragged around like a piece of luggage... Mom took us here all by herself. Where were you?

JANE: Don?

DAVID: Here, to get your papers and forms done.

DON: That long?!

DAVID: That was how long it took back then.
Took her forever to collect your documents.
It was a... complicated time in China.
The world was watching.
Traveling was hard.
Leaving was hard.
Everything was hard.

DON: You could've stayed.

DAVID: I had to take care of your grandpa, and we just opened the restaurant --

DON: Yeah, the restaurant. All you ever did was stay in the restaurant.

(A small beat.)

SCOTT: It's not really an easy job working the restaurant... the hours, the stress, the smell... it's really bad for your --

DON: I am talking to *my* father.

(Beat.)

DAVID: I wouldn't mind staying in China longer, but your mother... it was after you were born that she wanted to come here. She wanted you to see the world. I told her we'd be apart for quite some time, but I didn't see any fears or doubts on her face, I saw happiness and --

DON: She was trapped here in the house, all lonely and miserable. All she could do was wait for us to get home.

DAVID: That's got to be one of the most amazing feelings there ever has been -- waiting for someone you love to get home.
(beat)
I know I wasn't there... but I wrote her all the time...

(Lights up on YU QIN. She is murmuring the same content quietly in Chinese after DAVID.)

DAVID: Hey, do you know that China is eighteen hours ahead of Hawai'i? Do you know what that means? It means when you're having dinner, I'm just getting off work and heading home. When I'm on the freeway, I can always see the moon without even looking up. Island moon is always so beautiful, so bright that I lose my thought staring at it sometimes. You know what I was thinking about then? I was thinking if you had happened to be looking at the moon at that same time, it'd be as if I was looking at you.

YU QIN: 对了，你知道吗，中国的时间比夏威夷晚十八个小时。你知道那代表着什么吗？那代表着，当你在吃晚饭的时候，我刚下班，正往家里走呢。每当我开车在高速公路上时，不用抬头就能看见月亮。岛上的月亮那么美，那么亮，我看着看着就忘了自己还在开车。你知道那些时候我在想什么吗？我在想，如果当时的你也恰好抬头看着月亮的话，那就像是我在看着你一样。

(DAVID smiles. YU QIN smiles, too. Lights fade on YU QIN.)

JANE: Mom was always very happy, Don.

DON: But I never saw her happy.
I guess it was me.
It was me who always worried her... disappointed her,
failed her!

JANE: That's not true.

DON: I should have lied to her!
I should have told her I could fix it.
If I had followed her when she left the house --

JANE: That wasn't your fault!
It was dark.
The driver didn't see her –

DON: What if it wasn't like that?! What if she --

DAVID: Enough!
(beat)
Your mother loved you... very much. If she was still here
today, if she had enough time to think this through, I'm
more than convinced she would be proud of you! More
than anyone else could ever be.

DON: But are you?
(silence)
Dad, are you proud of me?
(silence)
Are you?

DAVID: *(painfully)* Sometimes, I wish you were not gay.

(DON lets out a long and bitter laugh of relief.)

DAVID: You can't ask me never to have that kind of
thought. You can't. It's selfish!

DON: I'm selfish?!

DAVID: You're my son, for as long as I live, I will try to understand you, I will try to accept you, and I will never stop wanting to protect you. But you just can't demand that in my whole life, I can't spend even one minute wondering what it's gotta be like to have a normal son. The life you could have had, the life I could have had.

DON: "Normal?"

DAVID: It doesn't mean I don't care about you -- it means I care about you so damn much that I don't want you to have a harder life. Do you think it's easy for people like you out there? Can you find anywhere other than big cities like New York just to be you? Every time I saw in the news about people getting beaten up just because they are holding hands, it scared me. We love you... I love you. You can't ask me to stop wishing you could ever have a normal life, a normal family, where you're not getting your heart broken by sleeping with someone else's husband, and someone else's father!
(silence, then quietly)
Excuse me.

(DAVID walks offstage. JANE wants to go check on him. SCOTT stops her.)

SCOTT: I'll check on him.
and...
I know it's
not my place to
but
...
...
never mind
...

(He exits. Silence. DON sits down. He looks at the mooncakes. All of a sudden, he stuffs them all in his mouth like there is an insatiable hunger in him.)

JANE: What's gotten into you?!

DON: *You* told me to talk to him. *You* said he could understand!

JANE: Can you blame him, for wanting you to be happy in the only way he knows how?

DON: If he can never be okay with it, at least he should stop pretending.

JANE: Why do you even care what he thinks of you? When did you ever give a fuck about what we think? You haven't even come back for / ten years!

DON: I couldn't stay in this house! Okay? I left because I kept hearing her voice when I was alone in the living room. I left because I could still see the blue and red ambulance lights flashing by even when I closed my eyes. I left because all I needed was a fucking hug but I looked at him and all I could see was disappointment.

JANE: Cut it out. Nobody's ever blamed you --

DON: That just made me blame myself even more. It's / killing me!

JANE: Then fucking do something. You don't get to cut yourself out then come back blaming us for not understanding you. It doesn't work like that! You stay and you do the work and you make people see you. What did you do?? You just packed up and left, and then out of nowhere you show up like nothing ever happened and you just walk around being mean and attacking everybody.

81

DON: That's the only way to get people to honestly talk about something in this house!

JANE: You wanna be honest? Fine. Let's be honest. I think you just want to pick fights because you want us to hate you, so you get to walk away guilt-free and never have to think about the family you left behind. I wanna be very clear. *You* abandoned us. It's not the other way around. It's never the other / way around.

DON: I didn't abandon anybody. He barely talked to me for that entire / year!

JANE: It was a difficult time. He didn't know how.

DON: You don't know!

JANE: What do you think, Don? I'm the sister. I'm the daughter. I was the only woman in the house. Yes, you lost your mother, he lost his wife, but did anyone care that I lost my mother too?! You took your sweet time mourning, while I took care of every other fucking thing!

DON: No one asked you to!

JANE: I had to! At least somebody in the house had to grow a pair!

(SCOTT enters. Beat.)

DON: Somebody in the house had to grow a pair, huh? When did you plan to tell me that you two were *fucking*?

SCOTT: Look --

DON: I'm asking HER.

JANE: I didn't mean to keep you in the dark. We just wanted to give it some more / time.

DON: You've got a goddamn tan line on your ring finger, Jane. How much more time do you need?!

JANE: You showed up at the door looking like you've already had a hell of tough time. I didn't want to upset you --

DON: Enough of that. Why is everyone trying to decide what's best for *me*??

JANE: I was just trying to... protect you.

DON: Really? Or were you just afraid that there's more to what I've told you about your fiancé?

JANE: That was your stupid crush. It didn't mean anything.

(Beat. DON looks at SCOTT.)

DON: Have you ever told her the time we got trapped in the rain?

SCOTT: What?

DON: Ka'au Crater Trail.

SCOTT: It was just a hike...

DON: A dangerous one. Three waterfalls, and hikers have to climb up the third one to get to the crater, but we never made it there.

SCOTT: Only because it started to rain.

DON: It rained like crazy, the streams were flooding. We had to crawl under some giant leaves.

SCOTT: To hide from the water!

DON: We took our shirts off and huddled together --

SCOTT: Because we were already soaked and cold!

DON: Cold? I don't think so, because when you held me in your arms, I felt like your whole body was / burning.

JANE: STOP!

DON: I thought there was nothing for you to be afraid of.

JANE: It wasn't like that... He told me.

SCOTT: Nothing happened!

DON: Nothing happened?

SCOTT: It was a million years ago, why does it still matter?!

DON: It was the moment I
It was the moment I knew
If that was the end of the world
I want the one sitting next to me to be
a guy
It was the moment I realized I had to tell them
The way you held me --

SCOTT: I held you because I was trying to keep you warm!

DON: Then why did you kiss me?!

SCOTT: I didn't. You kissed me --

DON: Why didn't you stop me then??

SCOTT: Because I knew you needed it!

(A beat.)

DON: What...?

SCOTT: I didn't know what it was, but I could feel you liked it. I didn't know what you wanted from me, but I knew I wanted that closeness. I understood how you felt - I had never really been close with anyone, never felt wanted. I didn't know what to do with my life, until I started working for your father. People liked me. You liked me! I was so scared if I said anything, I would just go back to being a stupid haole...

(A beat.)

DON: What am I, your training wheel?

SCOTT: No...!

DON: So what am I to you?

SCOTT: You're my friend.

DON: ... Fuck you.

SCOTT: You're my little brother.

DON: Fuck you! He's lying. He's a fucking LIAR!

JANE: Don, don't do this...

DON: What am I?
Huh?
WHAT AM I?!

(Suddenly, DON runs to SCOTT, and holds him in his
arms as tightly as he possibly can.

SCOTT tries to break the embrace, but DON won't let go.
Finally, SCOTT has to push him to the ground.)

SCOTT: Don... let go, please.
Don. Don. Don!
For God's sake
You're a man, Don.
GROW UP!! Will you??

(As DON falls unto the ground, YU QIN comes in. Sudden
lights shift. Reality breaks as the past bleeds into the present. JANE and SCOTT become the chorus of the memory
of YU QIN. They echo her. Suggested places to echo are
in bold. They are back at their final moment.)

YU QIN: 你醒醒吧，男人就该要有男人的样子！
[Wake up. **When will you act like a man?!**]

DON: I am almost eighteen. I know what I want.

YU QIN: 你好好听我说 –
[**Listen to me carefully--**]

DON: Please. No more talks. I can't take it anymore.

86

YU QIN: 妈妈只是想… talk… to you.

[Mom just want to **talk to you**.]

DON: You are not talking to me. You are brainwashing me!

YU QIN: 可我还等着有朝一日，你带女朋友回家呢！

[**I have been waiting** for the day when you bring home your girlfriend!]

我还等着做饭给她吃呢！

[**I have been waiting** to cook for her.]

DON: I could bring home a boyfriend and you can cook for him.

YU QIN: 那不一样。

[**It's not the same.**]

没有孩子今后老了怎么办？

[If you don't have kids what are you going to do when you get old?]

DON: Just because I... like guys doesn't mean I can't have kids.

YU QIN: 小孩子长大的时候怎么能没有妈呢？

[How can a child grow up without a mother around?]

DON: So? You raised me by yourself --

YU QIN: 你在怪我吗？

[**Are you blaming me?**]

87

DON: This is normal in America!

YU QIN: We don't come here so you do *this*!

DON: You brought me here. How could you expect me to not be free??

YU QIN: 我这是在叫你悬崖勒马！
[I'm trying to stop you from falling!]
[**Wǒ zhè shì zài jiào nǐ xuányálèmǎ**]

DON: I don't understand that word!

YU QIN: Fix it then!

DON: I can't!

YU QIN: **But you're a man...!!**

DON: STOP.
STOP STOP STOP.
STOP SAYING THAT TO ME.
WHAT DOES IT MEAN?
WHAT DOES IT FUCKING MEAN?
I AM A MAN.
YES. I AM A MAN.
BUT I AM JUST... A MAN!

(Beat. YU QIN leaves. DON watches her. There is nothing he can do except...

Lights shift, deafening sound of the rain goes on and on, as if it will never end.

Then, trees start to grow around him. Water dripping on him from overhead branches. He finds himself back at Ka'au Crater.

A younger SCOTT crawls in to sit with him. They are looking at the rain outside.)

SCOTT: We probably won't make it to the end today.
Do you think it will ever stop?
Hey, what if the crater gets full, like the water has no-where to go?
What if it's still an active volcano?
It's like a huge bowl of hot soup.
I'm hungry.
If it gets dark, we may have to spend the night here.
Aren't you a little scared?
But you're shaking.
Come.
Better?

Doesn't this feel like the end of the world?

(A kiss of gratitude. DON lets the memories go. Lights shift.)

13.

(Early morning. DON is alone with his suitcase. He finishes packing. JANE enters. She has her ring back on. Silence.)

JANE: Packed you some snacks. for the plane.

DON: Thank you.

89

(He doesn't take them. She goes to put them in his bag.)

JANE: It's a long flight. You're gonna need them.

DON: You know I can take the bus...

JANE: Pa wants to drive you.
…
I think you should let him.

(A silence.)

DON: I know what you're thinking...

JANE: What am I thinking...?

DON: "here he is, packing up and leaving again"

JANE: That's not what I'm thinking.

DON: Oh...?

JANE: I'm thinking... "He must make a shitload of money, changing his flight last-minute."

(Some laughs: soft, careful, but genuine.)

DON: I just
There're some stuff
In the city
I need to
take care of

JANE: Yeah. I'm sure.
So.
...

...
I know we both said
some things
Things we --

DON: I'm... glad you said them.

JANE: You are...?

DON: I thought I was out there
chasing something
but
all along
I was just
(escaping...)

(A beat.)

JANE: I know you thought
leaving would probably solve
everything
But I just think
when we have a connection with a place
it never really goes away
When you leave
you leave a piece of yourself there
And a piece of the place stays in you
and it grows
it just keeps growing and growing
And it has roots
And it grows deep
Mom once told me that
When I asked her
If she had ever missed China.

(Beat.)

DON: I
I'm sorry.
For

JANE: You're my brother.

DON: Right...

JANE: We'll miss you.

DON: Thank you.

(DAVID enters. He has car key in his hand. A beat.)

DAVID: Ready?

DON: Yeah.

DAVID: So...
do you wanna
see the new place?
we can stop by
show you your new room

DON: It's... the opposite direction of the airport...

DAVID: Okay...

DON: But
I
I want to come back to
help move
if I can
if you need me

DAVID: That's...
yeah
If you

(A beat. DON puts on his shoes.)

DAVID: Do you wanna drive?

DON: Huh?

DAVID: Feels nice.

DON: I've never really
And I don't actually
...
nobody drives in New York

DAVID: Do you still remember the first time I taught you how to drive, and we went all the way to the North Shore?

DON: It was a nice drive.

DAVID: You kept driving and driving, wanting to find the perfect beach, then all of a sudden, we were on Kame-hameha Highway heading downtown again. It was too late. We were stuck on that one-way road...

(He laughs a little.)

DON: I was scared to turn around... I had *just* learned how to drive.

(A beat.)

DAVID: Yeah...

(SCOTT enters with a dusty photo album. JANE take the album.)

93

JANE: here are some pictures
we took
the year we got here
I already packed it
but
thought maybe you can...

DON: Thank you...

(A beat. He takes it. They look at some pictures together.)

DAVID: Shall we?

(Everyone else leaves for the car.

DON holds the album in his hand.

He heads towards the door.

*The room transforms. Sounds of a banquet fill the air.
People laughing and talking in Chinese, wine glasses
clinking, kids crying and running around. The banquet.
The night they arrived in Hawai'i for the first time.*

He is five again.)

14.

*(Lights up on YU QIN. Noises of the banquet fill the air.
Everyone is there. She is happy, and a little drunk.)*

YU QIN: 什么？我才没醉！是你醉了！
[What? I'm not drunk. You're drunk!]

94

You! You drink too much! 啊？不行不行！我哪儿会唱什么歌呢？
[What? No way! I can't sing.]

你快住嘴，阿真。
[Shut up, Jane.]

Don't! No. No listen to her. 哎呀，我真的不会唱！
[I really can't sing!]

我叫雨琴又怎么样？又不可能唱得像雨那么好听。
[So what that I'm called "Yu Qin"? It's not like I can sing as beautiful as the sound when it is raining.]

Okay okay! 就唱一两句。
[Just one line or two then.]

不准笑我啊！
[Don't laugh at me!]
(clears her throat, about to sing)
真的不准笑啊！
[For real! Don't laugh.]
(singing slowly with an accent; a bit off-tune)
Fly me to the moon
Let me play among the stars
Let me see what spring is like
On a Jupiter and Mars
In other words, hold my hand
In other words, darling, kiss me
(crowd cheering; she shushes them)
No, not finish! 走开！
[Go away!]

95

(She laughs, and starts to drink. As she is drinking, noises of the banquet fade. A light comes up on DON. He looks at her in amazement. A burst of music and lights. She is the star. She climbs up on her chair, dances a little, then sings, in perfect English.)

YU QIN: Fill my heart with song
And let me sing for ever more
You are all I long for
All I worship and adore
In other words, please be true
In other words...
(beat; lights shift)
In other words...
I...

(Lights fade, music stops. A silence, DON is pulled back to reality. He studies the room, gets his suitcase, then heads to the door. As he is about to leave the house, she turns her head, and looks at him.

In the darkness, the last two notes of her unfinished song gently drop, clear and crisp, like the end of every rain.)

END OF PLAY.

NOTES

NOTES

NOTES

Made in the USA
Middletown, DE
16 January 2022

58848139R00056